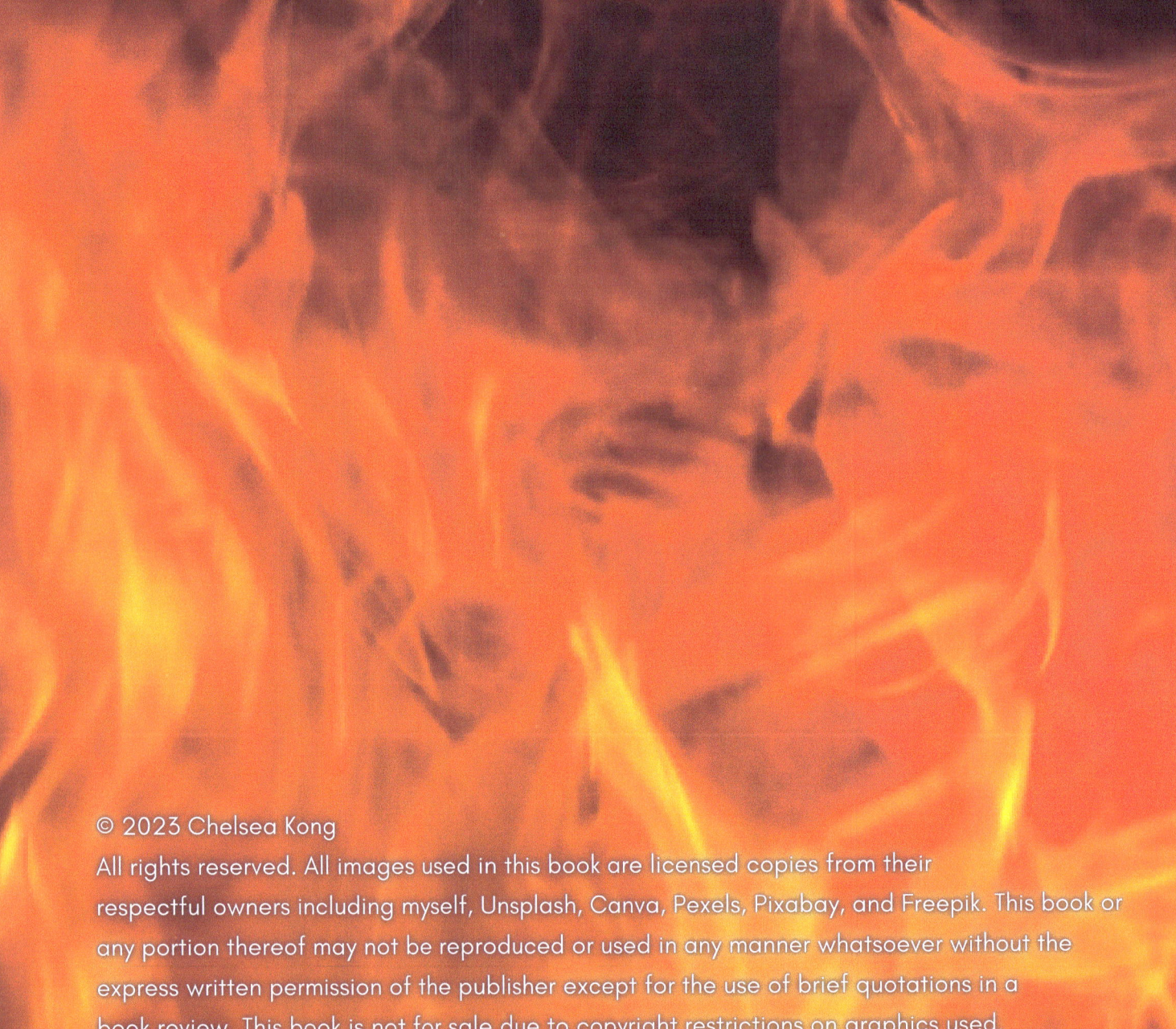

© 2023 Chelsea Kong

All rights reserved. All images used in this book are licensed copies from their respectful owners including myself, Unsplash, Canva, Pexels, Pixabay, and Freepik. This book or any portion thereof may not be reproduced or used in any manner whatsoever without the express written permission of the publisher except for the use of brief quotations in a book review. This book is not for sale due to copyright restrictions on graphics used.

Printed in 2023, Toronto, Ontario

ISBN: 978-1-990399-27-5

What is revival?
It is making something or someone important again.
It is to make something better.

What does it look like?
It is when many people are together in one place.
They are all doing the same things together for hours.

How does it begin?
God, Jesus, and the Holy Spirit must be first.
People don't think about time.

You and others seek God daily.
Always pray every day and meeting to pray.
Go to church every week and every meeting.

We must be sorry for what we have done.
Pray and obey God and stop doing evil ways.
Then God will hear, He will forgive our sin,
and heal our land. (2 Chronicles 7:14)

Open your heart and ask for more of Jesus.
Ask in faith for revival.
Stop the sin (all the wrong things you did).

Ask Jesus to help you stop doing evil.
Obey His Word every day.
Be holy and live right because He is Holy.

Ask Jesus to take out the evil things from you.
Stop all the bad words from your mouth.
Change your heart and make it full of love.

Forgive those who hurt you.
Forget what others did to you.
Bless and speak good to each other.

Peace, joy, and love with come into our heart.
You will be free from sin and feel His glory.
Share God's love with others.

Let others share God's Word.
Let others do what God tells them to do.
Thank God for them and pray to God to bless them.

Learn to wait in God's presence.
Listen to the Holy Spirit.
Keep your eyes on Jesus all the time.

Ask for the Holy Spirit to baptize you.
Believe and open your heart and speak with faith.
Let the words you do not know come out.

Speak in the Holy Spirit by the Holy Spirit.
Let Him speak of the future.
Let the Holy Spirit give you new gifts.

We need to love others like Jesus does.
Revival must come to the world.
Revival must happen in our life and church.

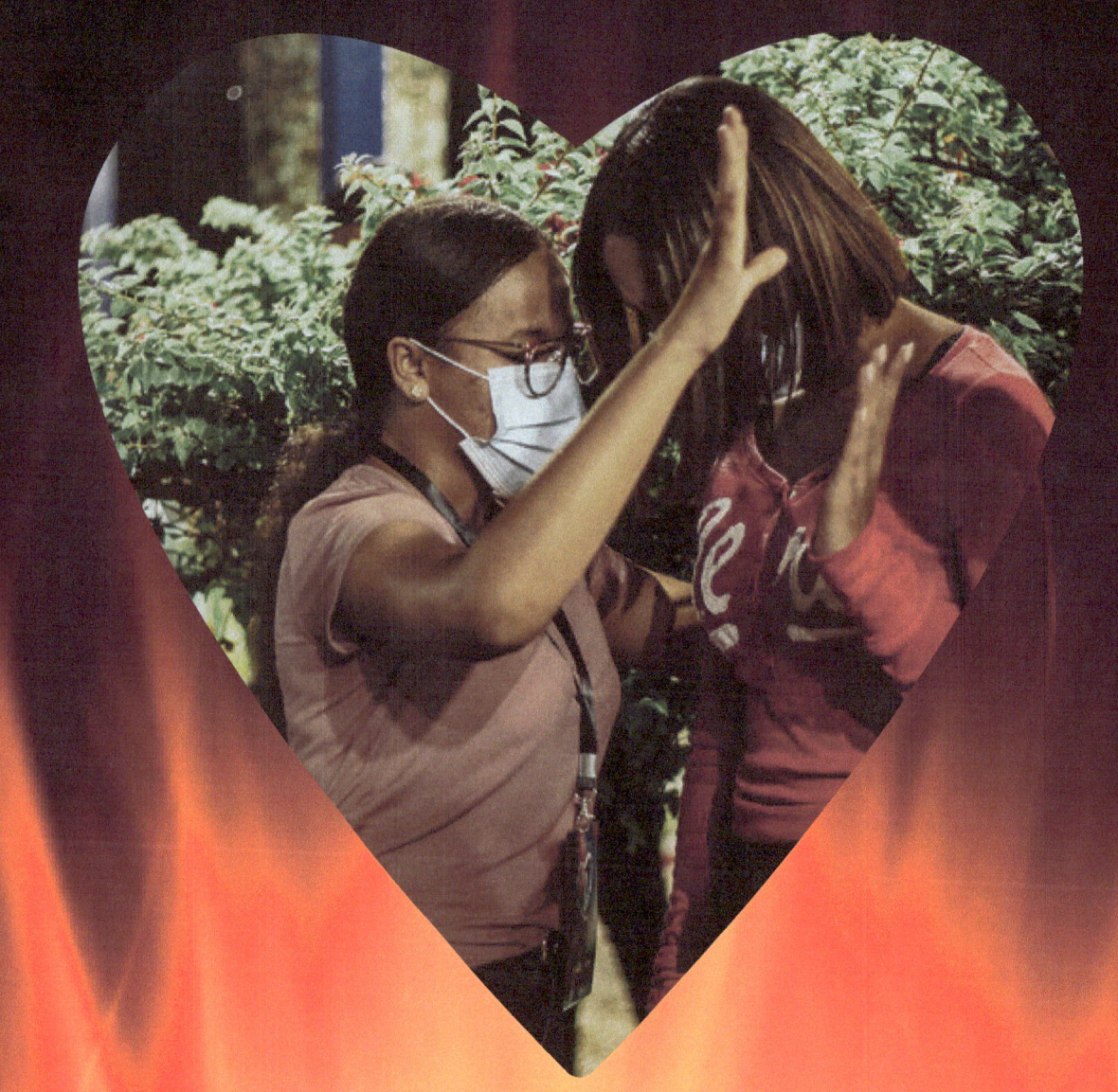

Holy Spirit touches your heart.
You want to keep on praying and seeking God.
He will give you a greater love for Jesus.

You keep praying and singing songs.
You will want to read the Bible.
You don't want to sin against God.

Pray for revival to come everywhere you go.
Pray for people to know Jesus.
You will want to meet every day and be with Jesus.

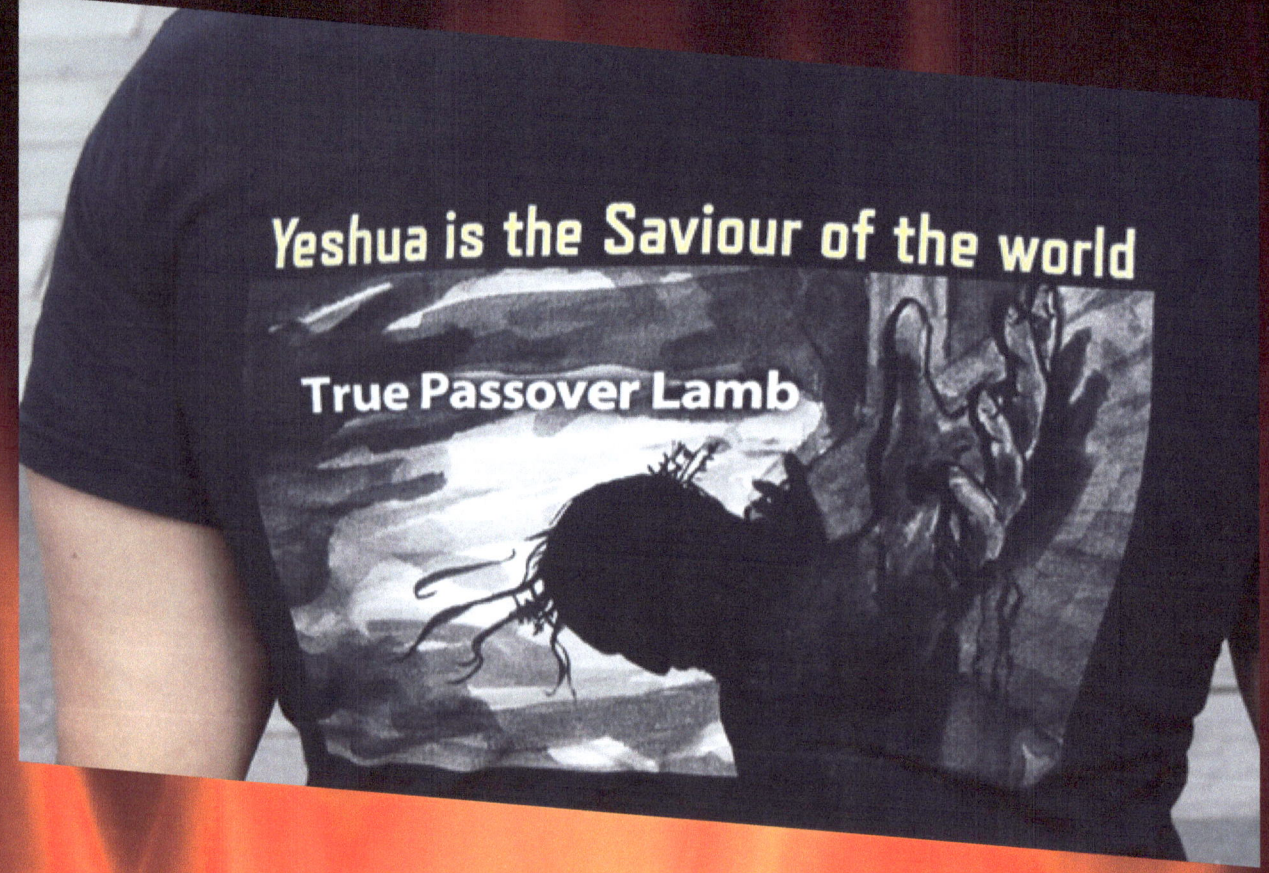

Fear God and not man.
Keep peace with others and agree with God.
Help those who have a need if you can.

You feel God's presence stronger.
Other people join you to sing and seek God.
They also pray, and God heals and does miracles.

Keep praising and dancing before Him.
Keep a pure and open heart.
Let God use you and do whatever He wants.

Share what Jesus did and let others do that.
Pray for healing for others.
People pray for each other.

Stay in worship with God with songs.
Thank God for healing, freedom, and bless Him.
Share Jesus and people get saved.

Tell others what Jesus did for you.
Be open to the Holy Spirit and wait.
Let the Holy Spirit tell you what to do and say.

Dance before the Lord and give thanks.
Rest in His presence.
Let the Lord work inside your heart.

Ask the Holy Spirit for a deeper love of God.
Ask for a new anointing.
Ask and receive the fire of the Holy Spirit.

Keep wanting the Lord every day and talking to Him. Ask for dreams, visions, and to speak into the future. Know what they mean and pray for them.

People will get baptized in water.
They will stay for hours with the Lord.
They may not want to eat or drink (fasting).

Train others to carry Jesus everywhere they go.
Stay in God's love and share His love with them.
Meet every week to worship, pray, and grow.

Remember, revival belongs to God.
Do not say that you made it happen.
Put God above yourself.

God's glory will come to the place where you meet.
There will be an increase because people will come.
You and others will increase too.

God will give you more than you want.
God will enjoy being with us and He lifts us up.
He will keep the revival, growing if we stay with Him.

God hates sin, and He will judge us.
Revival may not be the same as before.
God knows what is best.

In the book of Acts, the church is in revival. People gave to help others who have a need. They shared everything they had.

Peter told Ananias and Sapphira that they lied. They lied to the Holy Spirit, and they died. Then everyone feared God. (Acts 5:1-11)

Revival can be the love of God.
Revival can be a hot fire and the fear of God.
Be open to revival and do not judge it.

God will punish those who judge it.
They will get nothing good from Him.
Satan uses these people to cause trouble.

Do not listen to or answer the wicked.
Leave them to God and pray for them to repent.
Keep your heart right before God and He will judge.

You will save your life from evil.
You will keep it clean before God.
Then God will keep working in you and for you.

Revival will spread to many places.
Many people will come to Jesus.
God has a chose the number of people to be saved.
He will take us with Him to heaven.

SALVATION PRAYER

God, I know I sinned against you. Forgive me for the wrong that I have done. I believe that Jesus Christ died on the cross for me. That He rose from the grave so that after three days. I can have His long-lasting life. Come into my heart to be my Lord and Savior. I choose to turn away from my sins and I choose to follow you. Lead me to walk with you. Keep me safe and teach me your ways. Stop every bad thing in my life that has an open door to hurt me. Close those doors. Holy Spirit, fill me now in Jesus' name. Amen.

BAPTISM IN THE HOLY SPIRIT

Jesus, you are the one that fills me with Your Spirit. Come Holy Spirit and come into my life and fill me to overflow with Your presence. Come with your fire too. Thank you for the gift of tongues in Jesus' name. Amen.

Open your mouth and let the words come out that God gives you. It will be words that you don't know what they mean. You can ask God what it means. You need to let Him talk through you every day to grow this gift.

He will bring you closer to God and you will know Jesus more. You will have power from God to do great things and know things.

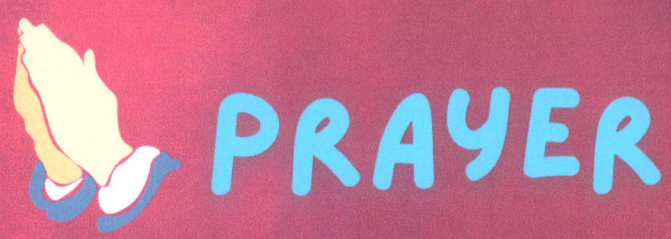

PRAYER

Father, thank you for the revival. Give me a heart for revival. Give me love for those who don't know you. I want to have your love for others. I give my life to you, Jesus. Take my life and use it for your glory. I am sorry for every time I did not obey you. Forgive me and heal my heart. Make me clean and change my heart. Give me a new mind to think the right way. I want revival for my family, home, church, school, and friends. I want revival for my city, country, and everyone in Jesus' name. Amen.

Message from the Author

Revival first starts with us. A few people come together to pray with Jesus. He gives us the heart for revival. We just need to obey Him and keep away from evil. Then we will see revival. Holy Spirit will give us the power and the strength to pray powerful prayers. He gives us the words to speak. He gives us what we need to tell others about Jesus. He also changes us. He reminds us when we sin. He is gentle and waits for us to follow. We must want Jesus more than anything in the world. He must be the first in our life. Do not judge how God does revival. It will be different. There is a revival of God's love and there is a revival that is like fire. It causes people to fear God and hate evil. In the book of Acts, Peter told Ananias and Sapphira that they lied to the Holy Spirit. God killed them. God will do this when people choose to sin when His a strong revival of His presence comes.

OTHER PRODUCTS

- Knowing God
- How to Hear God's Voice
- New Life in Jesus
- Loving Israel
- God's Gifts/Spiritual Talents
- Meeting God
- Word Power
- Fruit of the Spirit
- The Tabernacle
- Bride for Jesus
- A Life of Prayer
- Live Free
- Who am I in Jesus
- Walk in Love
- God's Favor
- Man of God
- Woman of God
- How to Use Money
- God's Wisdom
- Fasting
- See Jerusalem and Bethany
- First Fruit Offering
- Feast of Trumpets
- Day of Atonement
- Feast of Tabernacles
- Counting the Omer
- Festival of Lights
- See Galilee, Nazareth, and Tiberias
- Pentecost
- Glory, Presence, and Holy Spirit
- Live in God's Presence
- 31 Day Devotional
- Biblical Puzzle Book Vol 1-5
- Bible Puzzles for Young Children Book 1-3
- Biblical Puzzle for Children Books 1-3
- Hear God Speak
- Knowing Jesus
- Knowing Holy Spirit
- A Healthy Life and A Healthy Life Work Book
- Smokey the Cat
- Passover Unleavened Bread
- The Blessing
- Chelsea's Psalms and Poems
- Chelsea Learns Hebrew
- Give Thanks
- Thanksgiving

OTHER PRODUCTS

Teaching Series

How to Hear God's Voice Teaching Guide & Audio Book
Relationship with God, Jesus, Holy Spirit Guide
Knowing God, Jesus, Holy Spirit Guide & Audio Book
Flowing in the Prophetic

Teaching (Non-Sale on my website)

Purim
Passover
Resurrection

More books to come!

More books on Amazon, Kobo, and Barnes and Noble
https://chelseak532002550.wordpress.com/

Review

More books on Amazon, Kobo, and Barnes and Noble
https://www.amazon.com/author/chelseakong

Please leave a review and share with friends to help the author continue to write more books to reach more readers. Thank you so much for your support.

About
CHELSEA KONG

She is a writer, creative arts and digital media artist, skilled administration professional, and podcaster. Chelsea also served in a variety of roles, from audiovisual, photography, to assisting on the worship team, and ministry team. She also has a passion for families being united.

Chelsea has been a guest on Unity Live Radio, The Lady Tracey Show, and How to Live for Christ and is highly recommended by a Proud Christian blog. She is also a guest blogger. A few of her books have been featured in YourAuthorHub, etc. She graduated from Hotel and Restaurant Management, Digital Media Arts, Office Administration, Payroll Professional, and experience working with children. Chelsea lives in Toronto, Canada. She mainly writes children's books, stories, bridal writing, poems, lyrics for songs, words of encouragement, blessings, prayers, and jokes. The author of How to Hear the Voice of God, the Bridal Collection, Knowing God, etc. She also has her own Bible Puzzle books and other inspired products. Her podcast channel is called Chelsea K on Anchor, Spotify, and iTunes.

Please check my website to find out more:
https://chelseak532002550.wordpress.com/

www.ingramcontent.com/pod-product-compliance
Lightning Source LLC
Chambersburg PA
CBHW041413010526
44107CB00016B/1154